BinaryCoder X

Home based businesses

Dedication: Home-Based Businesses in 2024 by BinaryCoder X

To the innovators, the dreamers, and the creators who turn the familiar walls of home into the canvas of entrepreneurship. This guide is dedicated to those forging their path in the digital landscape, decoded by the spirit of BinaryCoder X.

Epigraph: Home-Based Businesses in 2024 by BinaryCoder X

"In the binary choices of opportunity, within the zeros and ones of innovation, emerges the blueprint of entrepreneurial triumph. Welcome to the realm where home and business converge—decoded by BinaryCoder X."

Contents

4.

5.

6.

7.

8.

9.

10.

11.

12.

13.

14.

15.

16.

17.

Foreword

Foreword: Home-Based Businesses in 2024 by BinaryCoder X

In the vast realm of entrepreneurship, where innovation meets determination, Home-Based Businesses in 2024 stands as a beacon guiding aspiring entrepreneurs through the ever-evolving landscape of possibilities. I am thrilled to pen this foreword for a guide that not only encapsulates the spirit of contemporary business but is also a testament to the transformative power embedded in the very concept of home-based entrepreneurship.

As BinaryCoder X, I've witnessed the rapid evolution of businesses influenced by technology, changing work dynamics, and a global shift towards remote work. The idea of operating a thriving venture from the confines of one's home has transcended mere convenience; it has become a powerful symbol of adaptability and empowerment.

This guide, penned with meticulous insight and practical wisdom, embarks on a journey through the diverse avenues of home-based businesses. Each chapter is a portal into a unique world of possibilities, from the artisanal charm of home bakeries to the strategic finesse of virtual assistants. The narrative weaves together the threads of creativity, strategy, and resilience that define successful home-based enterprises.

BinaryCoder X isn't just a pseudonym—it represents a mindset, a fusion of the digital and the entrepreneurial. In a world increasingly defined by zeros and ones, the guide navigates the binary code of home-based businesses, breaking down complexities into actionable steps. It invites entrepreneurs to not only decode the nuances of each venture but also to envision their home as a canvas for innovative and sustainable business practices.

As you embark on this exploration guided by BinaryCoder X, embrace the challenges and triumphs that come with the entrepreneurial journey. Whether you're a seasoned professional seeking a shift in work dynamics or a budding entrepreneur ready to carve your niche, this guide is a companion in your pursuit of home-based business success in 2024.

Let the pages ahead serve as a source of inspiration, a roadmap for strategic growth, and a reminder that within the binary choices of opportunities, your unique code holds the power to reshape your professional destiny. The future of home-based businesses awaits your imprint, and BinaryCoder X is here to guide you through the binary tapestry of entrepreneurial excellence.

May your journey be filled with innovation, resilience, and the unwavering belief that from the binary code emerges the blueprint of your entrepreneurial triumph.

BinaryCoder X

Preface

Preface: Home-Based Businesses in 2024

Welcome to the dynamic world of Home-Based Businesses in 2024. The landscape of entrepreneurship has evolved, and the concept of conducting business from the comfort of one's home has taken center stage. In this era of technological innovation, shifting work paradigms, and a renewed focus on work-life balance, the prospect of establishing and thriving in a home-based business has never been more enticing.

This guide serves as a compass through the diverse and exciting array of home-based business opportunities available in 2024. As we delve into each venture, envision the possibilities that await—from the aroma of freshly baked goods emanating from home bakeries to the artistic prowess showcased in virtual graphic design studios. The pages ahead unravel the secrets to success for those embarking on this entrepreneurial journey.

Each chapter unveils a distinct avenue, offering insights, strategies, and practical advice to transform your home into a bustling hub of creativity, productivity, and prosperity.

Whether you aspire to become a virtual assistant, embark on the journey of crafting handmade soaps, or provide language tutoring services from your study, this guide is your companion in navigating the nuanced terrain of home-based businesses.

In the age of connectivity and digital prowess, these ventures are not just about escaping the traditional office space; they are about embracing the freedom to shape your destiny, pursue your passions, and create a sustainable livelihood—all within the familiar walls of your home. As you flip through the chapters, let the possibilities unfold and inspire you to embark on a journey of entrepreneurship like never before.

Embrace the entrepreneurial spirit, harness the power of your home, and let this guide be the catalyst for turning your aspirations into a thriving reality. The world of home-based businesses in 2024 awaits your unique vision and the boundless potential within your living space. Are you ready to redefine your professional narrative and shape your own success story? The adventure begins now.

Acknowledgement

Acknowledgment: Home-Based Businesses in 2024 by BinaryCoder X

In the labyrinth of entrepreneurial endeavors, the creation of this guide, "Home-Based Businesses in 2024," has been an exhilarating exploration of possibilities, innovation, and the ever-changing dynamics of the business world. As BinaryCoder X, I extend my heartfelt gratitude to the individuals and elements that have contributed to the realization of this project.

First and foremost, my appreciation goes to the tireless entrepreneurs, both seasoned and aspiring, who form the heartbeat of the business landscape. Your courage to embark on the journey of home-based businesses inspires the very essence of this guide.

A special acknowledgment to the trailblazers in the entrepreneurial ecosystem, whose insights and experiences have shaped the content within these pages. Your wisdom has illuminated the path for those navigating the intricate terrain of home-based ventures.

I express sincere gratitude to the creative minds behind each home-based business featured in this guide. Your stories, strategies, and innovations serve as a source of inspiration for those seeking to redefine their professional narrative from the comfort of their homes.

To the unsung heroes of the digital era—virtual assistants, e-commerce enthusiasts, language tutors, and graphic designers—thank you for contributing to the rich tapestry of home-based entrepreneurship. Your roles are pivotal in showcasing the diverse and vibrant spectrum of possibilities.

I extend my appreciation to the readers who embark on this journey. Your curiosity and determination to explore the world of home-based businesses are the driving force behind the existence of this guide.

A heartfelt thank you to the team involved in the creation of this guide. Your dedication, creativity, and collaborative spirit have transformed ideas into a tangible resource for the entrepreneurial community.

Lastly, to the ever-evolving landscape of business and technology, thank you for being the canvas upon which innovative ventures unfold. The dynamic interplay of opportunities and challenges continues to fuel the spirit of entrepreneurship, and it is within this context that "Home-Based Businesses in 2024" finds its purpose.

As we navigate the binary choices and complexities of the entrepreneurial journey, let this guide be a compass, a companion, and a source of inspiration for your pursuit of success in home-based businesses.

BinaryCoder   X

1

Home bakery or catering service

Starting a home bakery or catering service can be an exciting venture that combines your passion for baking with the joy of sharing delicious creations with others. Here's a guide to help you embark on this delightful journey.

1. Passion and Expertise:

Begin with what you love. If baking is your passion, channel that enthusiasm into creating a home bakery. Whether it's cupcakes, cookies, or custom cakes, your love for baking will shine through in your products.

2. Legalities and Permits:

Before diving in, research and understand the legal requirements for operating a home-based food business in your area. This may include permits, licenses, and compliance with health and safety regulations. Check with local authorities to ensure you meet all necessary standards.

3. Define Your Niche:

Identify your specialty. Whether it's artisanal bread, vegan treats, or custom-designed cakes, having a niche can set you apart in a competitive market. Consider your target audience and tailor your offerings accordingly.

4. Quality Ingredients:

Invest in high-quality ingredients. The taste and quality of your baked goods or catering offerings will be a crucial factor in building a loyal customer base. Source fresh, local ingredients whenever possible to enhance the overall quality of your products.

5. Professional Presentation:

Presentation matters. Invest time in perfecting the aesthetics of your creations. A visually appealing product can attract customers and leave a lasting impression. Think about packaging and branding to make your home bakery visually appealing.

6. Build an Online Presence:

In the digital age, having a strong online presence is key. Create a website or use social media platforms to showcase your products. Share mouth-watering images, customer testimonials, and details about your offerings to engage potential customers.

7. Customer Engagement:

Connect with your customers. Building relationships with your customers can lead to repeat business and positive word-of-mouth. Engage with your audience through social media, respond to reviews, and consider loyalty programs to reward repeat customers.

8. Pricing Strategy:

Determine a fair pricing strategy. Factor in the cost of ingredients, your time, and overhead expenses. Research competitors' pricing in your area to ensure your prices are competitive while reflecting the quality of your products.

9. Test and Adapt:

Don't be afraid to experiment. Regularly introduce new items to your menu and gather feedback from your customers. This flexibility can help you adapt to changing tastes and preferences.

10. Marketing and Networking:

Market your home bakery through various channels. Attend local events, collaborate with other businesses, and utilize social media to expand your reach. Networking can open doors to partnerships and collaborations that boost your business.

Starting a home bakery or catering service requires dedication, creativity, and a commitment to quality. With the right mix of passion and business acumen, you can turn your love for baking into a thriving venture that brings joy to your customers and fulfillment to your entrepreneurial spirit.

2

Personalized Gift Shop

2. Personalized Gift Shop:

Embarking on a journey to run a personalized gift shop from home opens up a world of creativity and meaningful connections with customers. Here's a guide to help you carve your niche in this heartfelt industry.

1. Discover Your Passion:

Identify your passion within the personalized gift realm. Whether it's custom-made jewelry, monogrammed items, or personalized home decor, find a niche that resonates with your interests and skills.

2. Legal Considerations:

Understand the legal aspects of operating a personalized gift shop from home. Research local business regulations, licensing requirements, and any permits needed. This is especially important if you're customizing products or handling sensitive materials.

3. Build an Online Presence:

Create a compelling online platform for your personalized gift shop. Develop a user-friendly website showcasing your products and offering a seamless shopping experience. Leverage social media platforms to share behind-the-scenes glimpses, customer testimonials, and engage with your audience.

4. Diverse Product Range:

Diversify your product offerings. Provide a range of personalized items to cater to different tastes and occasions. This could include personalized mugs, engraved jewelry, custom-made clothing, or even unique artwork. Offering variety ensures a broader appeal and attracts a wider customer base.

5. Quality Materials and Craftsmanship:

Ensure that your personalized gifts are crafted from high-quality materials. The longevity and quality of your products will contribute to customer satisfaction and positive reviews.

Emphasize the craftsmanship behind each personalized item, highlighting the care and attention to detail involved.

6. Customization Options:

Offer a range of customization options. This could include different fonts, colors, or even the option for customers to submit their own designs. Providing a personalized experience enhances the emotional connection customers have with your products, making them more likely to return and recommend your shop.

7. Packaging and Presentation:

Pay attention to packaging. The unboxing experience is crucial, especially when dealing with personalized gifts. Consider using eco-friendly materials and design packaging that complements the sentimental nature of your products. A beautifully presented gift adds an extra layer of joy for the recipient.

8. Marketing Strategies:

Implement effective marketing strategies. Utilize social media advertising, influencer collaborations, and email marketing to promote your personalized gift shop. Consider creating seasonal promotions or discounts to attract new customers and retain existing ones.

9. Customer Engagement:

Encourage customer feedback and engagement. Create a community around your brand by showcasing customer testimonials and featuring user-generated content. Engaging with your audience builds trust and loyalty, turning one-time buyers into repeat customers.

10. Stay Trendy and Timeless:

Keep an eye on industry trends while maintaining a timeless appeal. Balancing current trends with timeless designs ensures your personalized gift shop stays relevant and appealing to a wide audience. Stay open to evolving your product line to meet changing consumer preferences.

Running a personalized gift shop from home allows you to infuse your personality into each creation. By combining passion, craftsmanship, and strategic business practices, you can create a unique and thriving business that brings joy to both you and your customers.

3

Home Daycare or Pet Sitting

3. Home Daycare or Pet Sitting:

Transforming your home into a daycare for children or a haven for pets can be a fulfilling venture that combines care, responsibility, and the comforts of home. Here's a guide to embark on this nurturing journey.

1. Legal and Safety Compliance:

Begin by researching and complying with local regulations for home-based daycare or pet sitting services. This may involve obtaining licenses, adhering to safety standards, and possibly passing inspections. Prioritize the safety and well-being of the children or pets in your care.

2. Create a Welcoming Space:

Designate a space in your home that is safe and welcoming for children or pets. Ensure that the environment is childproofed or pet-friendly, with appropriate toys, furnishings, and safety measures in place. A well-thought-out space contributes to a positive experience for both the clients and their loved ones.

3. Establish Policies and Procedures:

Clearly define your policies and procedures. Communicate expectations with parents or pet owners regarding drop-off and pick-up times, fees, emergency procedures, and any specific rules you have in place. Having transparent guidelines helps set expectations and fosters trust with your clients.

4. Develop Age-Appropriate Programs:

For daycare services, tailor age-appropriate programs and activities for the children in your care. This could include educational play, arts and crafts, and outdoor activities. For pet sitting, design personalized care routines, ensuring that each pet receives the attention and activities they need.

5. Marketing and Networking:

Create a strong online presence to market your home daycare or pet sitting services. Build a professional website, leverage social media platforms, and consider partnerships with local pet stores or parenting groups to increase visibility. Positive reviews and word-of-mouth referrals are powerful in this industry.

6. Obtain Necessary Certifications:

Consider obtaining relevant certifications such as CPR and first aid training. This adds an extra layer of professionalism to your services and assures parents or pet owners that you prioritize the safety and well-being of those in your care.

7. Health and Nutrition Considerations:

For daycare services, pay attention to health and nutrition. Provide balanced meals and snacks, accommodating any dietary restrictions or allergies. Hygiene practices are crucial in a daycare setting. Similarly, for pet sitting, be mindful of dietary needs, exercise requirements, and any medical considerations for the animals in your care.

8. Build Trusting Relationships:

Foster trusting relationships with clients. Regularly communicate with parents or pet owners about their children or pets' well-being. Provide updates, share photos, and be responsive to any concerns or questions. Building a strong rapport contributes to long-lasting relationships and repeat business.

9. Pricing Structure:

Establish a fair and competitive pricing structure for your daycare or pet sitting services. Consider factors such as the level of care provided, additional services offered, and local market rates. Transparent pricing helps potential clients understand the value you bring to the table.

10. Stay Informed and Adaptable:

Stay informed about childcare or pet care best practices. Attend relevant workshops or conferences to stay updated on industry trends and regulations. Be adaptable to the evolving needs of your clients, adjusting your programs or services accordingly.

Transforming your home into a daycare or pet sitting service requires a blend of compassion, organization, and professionalism. By prioritizing safety, communication, and quality care, you can create a nurturing environment that becomes a trusted haven for children or pets in your community.

4

Plant Nursery or Gardening Services

4. Plant Nursery or Gardening Services:

Establishing a plant nursery or offering gardening services from home is a green and rewarding business venture. Here's a guide to help you cultivate success in the world of plants and gardening.

1. Passion for Plants:

Begin with a genuine passion for plants and gardening. Your enthusiasm will be evident in the care you provide to your plants and the advice you offer to customers. Whether you're growing ornamental plants, herbs, or vegetables, your love for gardening will be a driving force.

2. Research and Planning:

Conduct thorough research on the types of plants that thrive in your local climate. Plan your nursery layout, considering sunlight, water requirements, and space allocation. Understanding the specific needs of different plants ensures a healthy and diverse inventory.

3. Obtain Necessary Permits:

Check local regulations regarding operating a plant nursery from home. Secure any necessary permits or licenses, especially if you plan to sell plants. Compliance with local laws ensures a smooth operation and builds trust with customers.

4. Quality Plants and Supplies:

Focus on offering high-quality plants and gardening supplies. Partner with reputable suppliers for seeds, soil, and other essentials. Healthy and vibrant plants will attract customers and encourage repeat business. Consider offering advice on plant care to enhance customer satisfaction.

5. Create a Green Oasis:

Design an inviting and well-organized space for your nursery. Arrange plants aesthetically, making it easy for customers to explore and choose. Consider creating themed sections, such as "Shade Lovers" or "Drought-Tolerant Plants," to guide customers based on their specific needs.

6. Educational Workshops:

Offer educational workshops or tutorials on gardening. Share your expertise on plant care, gardening techniques, and landscape design. This not only adds value to your business but also positions you as a knowledgeable resource in your community.

7. Online Presence:

Build an online presence to showcase your plant nursery. Create a website with information on available plants, gardening tips, and contact details. Leverage social media platforms to share updates, gardening inspiration, and engage with your audience. Consider an online store for plant sales.

8. Custom Plant Arrangements:

Differentiate your business by offering custom plant arrangements. Create personalized garden designs based on customer preferences and the specific conditions of their outdoor space. This adds a personalized touch to your services and caters to customers looking for unique garden solutions.

9. Seasonal Promotions:

Implement seasonal promotions to attract customers during peak gardening times. Consider offering discounts on specific plant varieties, bundle deals, or promotions tied to gardening seasons. Seasonal marketing keeps your business dynamic and aligns with customers' changing needs.

10. Community Engagement:

Engage with the local community. Participate in community events, collaborate with local businesses, and support gardening initiatives. Building a sense of community around your plant nursery fosters customer loyalty and strengthens your brand presence.

Cultivating a successful plant nursery or gardening service from home requires a blend of horticultural knowledge, business acumen, and a genuine love for plants. By providing quality plants, fostering community engagement, and adapting to seasonal demands, you can turn your green passion into a flourishing business.

5

Fitness or Yoga Studio (Converted Home Space)

5. Fitness or Yoga Studio (Converted Home Space):

Transforming your home into a fitness or yoga studio allows you to share your passion for health and wellness while providing a personalized and comfortable space for clients. Here's a guide to help you establish a thriving home-based fitness or yoga business.

1. Certification and Training:

Obtain the necessary certifications and training in fitness instruction or yoga teaching. This not only enhances your credibility but also ensures that you can provide safe and effective workouts or yoga sessions for your clients.

2. Design a Dedicated Space:

Create a dedicated and inviting space within your home for fitness or yoga sessions. Ensure ample space for movement, good ventilation, and an aesthetically pleasing environment. Consider adding mirrors, appropriate flooring, and calming elements for yoga sessions.

3. Legal Considerations:

Check local regulations and zoning laws regarding operating a fitness or yoga studio from home. Obtain any required permits or licenses, and comply with safety and health standards. Ensuring legal compliance builds trust with clients and helps you run a legitimate business.

4. Personalized Programs:

Offer personalized fitness or yoga programs tailored to the individual needs and goals of your clients. Consider providing one-on-one sessions or small group classes to maintain a personalized and focused approach. Catering to the unique needs of each client sets your business apart.

5. Online Presence:

Establish a strong online presence to attract clients. Create a professional website detailing your services, qualifications, and class schedules. Utilize social media platforms to share workout tips, yoga poses, and testimonials. Consider offering online classes for those who prefer remote sessions.

6. Equipment and Amenities:

Invest in quality fitness or yoga equipment. Ensure you have the necessary props, mats, and accessories to create a well-equipped studio space. The availability of amenities like changing areas and water stations contributes to a positive client experience.

7. Class Variety:

Diversify your class offerings to cater to different fitness levels and preferences. Consider including various types of workouts or yoga styles, such as strength training, HIIT, or meditation sessions. Offering a variety keeps clients engaged and attracts a broader audience.

8. Pricing Structure:

Develop a transparent and competitive pricing structure. Consider offering package deals, memberships, or class bundles to accommodate different budgets. Clearly communicate the value of your services, highlighting the personalized attention and expertise you provide.

9. Client Engagement:

Foster a sense of community and engagement among your clients. Encourage feedback, host fitness challenges, and create a supportive online or in-person community. Building strong connections with your clients enhances retention and promotes positive word-of-mouth marketing.

10. Continuous Education:

Stay updated with the latest fitness or yoga trends and techniques. Attend workshops, webinars, or courses to enhance your skills and offer innovative sessions. Being well-informed positions you as a reliable and knowledgeable fitness or yoga instructor.

Establishing a fitness or yoga studio from home requires a blend of expertise, dedication, and a customer-centric approach. By creating a welcoming space, offering personalized programs, and staying connected with your clients, you can build a successful home-based business that promotes health and well-being in your community.

6

Beauty Salon or Spa Services

6. Beauty Salon or Spa Services:

Turning your home into a beauty salon or spa offers a luxurious and personalized experience for clients seeking relaxation and self-care. Here's a guide to help you set up and run a successful home-based beauty business.

1. Licensing and Certification:

Ensure you have the necessary licenses and certifications required to offer beauty or spa services. This may include certifications in cosmetology, esthetics, or massage therapy, depending on the services you plan to provide.

2. Design a Comfortable Space:

Create a dedicated and comfortable space within your home for beauty treatments. Consider factors like lighting, decor, and ambient music to enhance the overall experience. Ensure you have proper equipment and hygiene practices in place.

3. Legal Compliance:

Research and adhere to local regulations governing home-based beauty services. Obtain any required permits or licenses, and comply with health and safety standards. This not only ensures legal compliance but also builds trust with clients.

4. Services Menu:

Offer a comprehensive menu of services. This could include facials, massages, manicures, pedicures, hair styling, or any other beauty treatments you specialize in. Providing a variety of services allows you to cater to different client preferences.

5. Online Booking System:

Implement an online booking system to streamline appointment scheduling. This makes it convenient for clients to book sessions and allows you to manage your schedule efficiently. Consider offering flexible hours, including evenings and weekends, to accommodate diverse schedules.

6. High-Quality Products:

Invest in high-quality beauty products. The use of premium skincare, haircare, and beauty products enhances the effectiveness of your treatments and contributes to a luxurious experience for clients. Be transparent about the products you use to build trust.

7. Personalized Consultations:

Conduct personalized consultations with clients before each treatment. Understand their specific needs, preferences, and any skin or health concerns. Tailoring your services to individual clients ensures a customized and satisfying experience.

8. Marketing and Branding:

Create a strong brand identity and market your services effectively. Develop a professional website showcasing your services, prices, and contact information. Utilize social media platforms to share before-and-after photos, client testimonials, and promotions.

9. Client Loyalty Programs:

Implement client loyalty programs to reward repeat customers. Offer discounts, free treatments, or exclusive perks for clients who frequent your beauty salon or spa. Building loyalty enhances customer retention and encourages referrals.

10. Stay Informed About Trends:

Stay informed about the latest beauty trends, techniques, and product innovations. Attend industry events, workshops, or online courses to stay updated. Offering trendy and innovative services keeps your business competitive and attracts clients seeking the latest beauty offerings.

Establishing a beauty salon or spa at home requires a blend of technical expertise, creativity, and a commitment to exceptional customer service. By creating a relaxing environment, offering a diverse range of services, and staying current with industry trends, you can build a thriving home-based beauty business that leaves clients pampered and satisfied.

7

Home-based Photography Studio

7. Home-based Photography Studio:

Transforming a part of your home into a photography studio provides a creative space for capturing memorable moments. Whether you specialize in portraits, product photography, or artistic compositions, here's a guide to help you build and run a successful home-based photography business.

1. Specialization and Equipment:

Define your niche in photography. Whether it's family portraits, newborn photography, or commercial product shoots, having a specialization helps you target a specific audience. Invest in high-quality photography equipment suited to your chosen niche.

2. Design a Functional Studio Space:

Create a dedicated space within your home for your photography studio. Consider factors like lighting, background options, and sufficient space for your equipment and subjects. A well-designed studio contributes to a professional and organized workflow.

3. Legal Considerations:

Research and comply with legal requirements for operating a home-based photography studio. Check zoning regulations, obtain necessary permits, and ensure you have liability insurance. Addressing legal considerations from the start establishes a solid foundation for your business.

4. Portfolio Development:

Build a strong portfolio showcasing your best work. Display a variety of images that highlight your skills and style. A compelling portfolio serves as a visual resume and helps attract potential clients.

5. Online Presence:

Establish a strong online presence to showcase your portfolio and services. Create a professional website with a portfolio gallery, contact information, and details about your photography packages. Utilize social media platforms to share your work and engage with your audience.

6. Marketing and Networking:

Implement marketing strategies to reach potential clients. Utilize online advertising, collaborate with local businesses, and attend community events to promote your photography services. Networking within the community can lead to valuable partnerships and referrals.

7. Client Communication:

Prioritize effective communication with clients. Clearly outline your services, pricing, and any specific requirements for photo sessions. Respond promptly to inquiries and maintain open communication to build trust and satisfaction.

8. Pricing Structure:

Develop a transparent and competitive pricing structure for your photography services. Consider factors such as session duration, photo editing, and additional services. Clearly communicate your pricing on your website and marketing materials.

9. Customer Experience:

Focus on providing an exceptional customer experience. Ensure your clients feel comfortable and valued during photo sessions. Deliver high-quality edited images promptly, and offer personalized touches to enhance the overall experience.

10. Continuous Learning:

Stay updated with the latest photography trends, techniques, and equipment. Attend workshops, online courses, or photography conferences to enhance your skills. Continuous learning not only improves your craft but also keeps your business fresh and competitive.

Establishing a home-based photography studio requires a combination of artistic talent, technical proficiency, and effective business practices. By specializing in a niche, creating a functional studio space, and prioritizing customer satisfaction, you can build a thriving photography business that captures the essence of life's special moments.

8

Candle or Soap Making Business

8. Candle or Soap Making Business:

Creating a home-based business focused on crafting candles or soaps provides an avenue for artistic expression and a unique product offering. Here's a guide to help you light the way in the world of handmade candles or soaps.

1. Learn the Craft:

Begin by learning the art and science of candle or soap making. Understand different techniques, materials, and safety measures involved in the process. Online courses, workshops, and experimenting with small batches will help you hone your skills.

2. Designate a Workspace:

Create a dedicated workspace in your home for candle or soap making. Ensure good ventilation, organize your materials, and invest in the necessary equipment. A well-organized workspace contributes to a smooth and efficient production process.

3. Source Quality Materials:

Invest in high-quality materials for your candles or soaps. This includes waxes, fragrances, dyes, molds, and any other essential components. Using premium materials ensures a superior final product that delights your customers.

4. Develop Unique Products:

Differentiate your business by developing unique and distinctive candle or soap designs. Experiment with various scents, colors, shapes, and packaging. Offering a variety of products allows you to cater to diverse preferences and attract a broader customer base.

5. Compliance and Safety:

Understand and comply with safety regulations for candle and soap making. This may involve labeling requirements, safety data sheets, and adherence to specific guidelines. Prioritize customer safety and satisfaction by following industry standards.

6. Build an Online Presence:

Create an online platform to showcase your handmade candles or soaps. Develop a user-friendly website with high-quality images, product descriptions, and an easy ordering system. Leverage social media to share behind-the-scenes content, customer testimonials, and promotions.

7. Packaging and Branding:

Invest in appealing packaging that reflects the quality and uniqueness of your products. Thoughtful and aesthetically pleasing packaging contributes to the overall customer experience. Develop a brand identity that sets your handmade creations apart in the market.

8. Pricing Strategy:

Determine a pricing strategy that covers your production costs and provides a reasonable profit margin. Consider factors such as material costs, time invested, and market demand. Transparent pricing helps customers understand the value of your handcrafted items.

9. Marketing and Collaborations:

Implement marketing strategies to promote your candle or soap business. Collaborate with local shops, markets, or online platforms to expand your reach. Engage with your audience through social media, and consider hosting workshops or tutorials to share your craft.

10. Customer Engagement:

Foster a sense of community among your customers. Encourage feedback, run contests, or offer loyalty programs. Building a relationship with your audience fosters repeat business and word-of-mouth referrals.

Starting a candle or soap making business from home allows you to turn your passion for crafting into a thriving enterprise. By focusing on quality, creativity, and effective marketing, you can create products that illuminate the lives of your customers and set your business apart in the handmade market.

9

Mobile Car Detailing

9. Mobile Car Detailing:

Bringing the car detailing service directly to your customers offers convenience and personalized care for their vehicles. Here's a guide to help you rev up a successful mobile car detailing business from the comfort of your home.

1. Equip Your Mobile Unit:

Invest in high-quality car detailing equipment and supplies. Ensure your mobile unit is well-equipped with water tanks, power washers, cleaning solutions, and other tools necessary for comprehensive car detailing. A fully-equipped mobile unit allows you to offer a range of services at your clients' location.

2. Legal and Environmental Compliance:

Research and comply with local regulations regarding water usage, chemical disposal, and permits for operating a mobile car detailing service. Ensure that your business practices are environmentally friendly and adhere to local laws.

3. Set Clear Service Packages:

Define and communicate clear service packages for your mobile car detailing business. Offer a range of packages that cater to different customer needs, from basic exterior cleaning to full interior detailing. Clearly outline what each package includes to manage customer expectations.

4. Build a Professional Image:

Create a professional image for your mobile car detailing business. Develop a logo, branding materials, and a professional website. Presenting a polished image builds trust with potential clients and sets the stage for a high-quality service.

5. Mobile Appointments and Scheduling:

Implement a system for mobile appointments and scheduling. Utilize technology to streamline the booking process, whether through a dedicated app, website, or phone call.

Efficient scheduling ensures you can optimize your time and serve more clients.

6. Eco-Friendly Products:

Consider using eco-friendly and biodegradable car cleaning products. Not only does this appeal to environmentally conscious customers, but it also aligns your business with sustainable practices. Clearly communicate your commitment to eco-friendly detailing.

7. Marketing Strategies:

Develop effective marketing strategies to promote your mobile car detailing services. Utilize local advertising, social media platforms, and partnerships with local businesses. Offer promotions for first-time customers and loyalty programs to encourage repeat business.

8. Focus on Customer Satisfaction:

Prioritize customer satisfaction in every detail of your service. Ensure thorough and meticulous cleaning, address customer concerns promptly, and go the extra mile to exceed expectations. Positive customer experiences lead to repeat business and positive word-of-mouth referrals.

9. Networking with Auto Businesses:

Network with local auto dealerships, car rental companies, and other businesses in the automotive industry. Establish partnerships for discounted services or referrals. Networking within the automotive community can open up additional opportunities for your mobile car detailing business.

10. Continuous Improvement:

Stay informed about the latest car detailing techniques, products, and industry trends. Attend workshops, read industry publications, and seek opportunities for continuous improvement. Staying updated ensures your services remain competitive and of high quality.

Launching a mobile car detailing business from home allows you to combine your passion for cars with the flexibility of a mobile service. By focusing on professionalism, environmental considerations, and customer satisfaction, you can drive your business toward success.

45

10

Home-based Auto Repair

10. Home-based Auto Repair:

Offering auto repair services from home provides a convenient and personalized solution for car owners. Here's a guide to help you kickstart and navigate a successful home-based auto repair business.

1. Obtain Necessary Certifications:

Ensure you have the required certifications for auto repair. Depending on your location, this may involve obtaining an Automotive Service Excellence (ASE) certification or complying with other local regulations. Certification adds credibility to your services.

2. Design a Functional Workspace:

Create a dedicated and well-organized workspace for auto repairs within your home. Ensure you have the necessary tools, equipment, and safety measures in place. A functional workspace contributes to efficiency and a professional image.

3. Legal Compliance:

Research and comply with local regulations governing home-based auto repair businesses. This may include zoning laws, permits, and environmental regulations. Adhering to legal requirements ensures a smooth operation and builds trust with clients.

4. Services Offered:

Clearly define the auto repair services you offer. Whether it's routine maintenance, diagnostics, or specific repairs, communicate your expertise to potential clients. Having a clear list of services helps customers understand the scope of your capabilities.

5. Online Presence:

Establish an online presence to promote your home-based auto repair business. Create a professional website detailing your services, prices, and contact information. Utilize social media platforms to share your expertise, client testimonials, and promotions.

6. Mobile Repairs:

Consider offering mobile repair services for minor repairs or maintenance tasks. This provides added convenience for clients who may prefer repairs at their location. Clearly communicate the scope of mobile services and any associated fees.

7. Transparent Pricing:

Develop a transparent pricing structure for your auto repair services. Clearly outline costs for common repairs, diagnostics, and labor. Transparency in pricing builds trust with customers and helps them make informed decisions.

8. Networking with Local Businesses:

Network with local businesses in the automotive industry. Establish partnerships with auto parts suppliers, towing services, or other businesses that can complement your services. Collaborations can lead to referrals and a broader client base.

9. Build Customer Trust:

Focus on building trust with your customers. Provide accurate estimates, explain repairs in understandable terms, and be transparent about the process. Trustworthy and reliable services lead to repeat business and positive word-of-mouth referrals.

10. Stay Informed and Upgrade Skills:

Stay informed about the latest developments in auto repair technology, tools, and industry trends. Attend workshops, webinars, and training programs to upgrade your skills. Keeping up with advancements ensures your services remain competitive and up-to-date.

Starting a home-based auto repair business requires a combination of technical expertise, legal compliance, and effective communication. By offering transparent services, building trust with customers, and staying informed about industry changes, you can create a successful and reputable home-based auto repair business.

11

Home-based Tutoring or Educational Services

11. Home-based Tutoring or Educational Services:

Transforming your home into a tutoring center offers personalized educational support to students. Here's a guide to help you create a thriving home-based tutoring or educational services business.

1. Identify Areas of Expertise:

Determine the subjects or areas in which you excel and can offer effective tutoring. Whether it's math, science, language arts, or test preparation, focusing on your strengths enhances your ability to provide valuable assistance.

2. Educational Credentials:

Highlight your educational credentials and expertise in the subjects you plan to tutor. Share your qualifications on your website or marketing materials to build trust with potential clients and parents.

3. Design a Comfortable Learning Space:

Create a comfortable and well-equipped learning space within your home. Ensure good lighting, a quiet environment, and resources such as textbooks, writing materials, and a computer. A conducive learning space contributes to a positive educational experience.

4. Legal Considerations:

Understand and comply with legal considerations for offering educational services from home. This may involve checking local regulations, obtaining necessary certifications, and adhering to any specific requirements for tutoring businesses.

5. Online or In-Person Tutoring:

Decide whether you'll offer in-person tutoring, online sessions, or a combination of both. With the rise of online education, having the flexibility to cater to different preferences can expand your reach and accommodate diverse student needs.

6. Develop Customized Learning Plans:

Create customized learning plans for each student based on their strengths, weaknesses, and learning styles. Tailoring your approach ensures that students receive targeted support, leading to better academic performance.

7. Set Clear Pricing and Policies:

Define your pricing structure and policies for cancellations, rescheduling, and payment methods. Clear communication about costs and expectations helps build a professional and transparent relationship with parents and students.

8. Utilize Educational Technology:

Incorporate educational technology tools to enhance your tutoring sessions. Platforms for virtual learning, interactive resources, and educational apps can supplement your teaching methods and engage students in the learning process.

9. Marketing Strategies: Implement effective marketing strategies to attract students. Create a professional website with details about your tutoring services, educational background, and testimonials. Utilize local advertising, social media, and partnerships with schools to reach your target audience.

10. Parent and Student Communication:

Maintain open communication with parents and students. Provide regular updates on progress, areas of improvement, and any additional resources that can support their learning outside of tutoring sessions. Building strong relationships with parents fosters trust and satisfaction.

11. Continuous Professional Development:

Stay informed about educational trends, curriculum changes, and teaching methodologies. Attend workshops, conferences, or online courses to continuously improve your tutoring skills. Keeping up with advancements in education ensures you provide high-quality support to your students.

Creating a home-based tutoring or educational services business requires a commitment to personalized learning, effective communication, and ongoing professional development. By leveraging your expertise, embracing educational technology, and building strong relationships with students and parents, you can make a positive impact on the academic success of your students.

12

Home-based Graphic Design Studio

12. Home-based Graphic Design Studio:

Establishing a graphic design studio from home allows you to showcase your creativity and serve clients with diverse design needs. Here's a guide to help you kickstart and manage a successful home-based graphic design business.

1. Define Your Niche:

Identify your niche within the graphic design realm. Whether it's logo design, branding, web design, or illustration, specializing in a specific area allows you to target a particular client base and excel in your chosen field.

2. Acquire Necessary Software and Tools:

Invest in professional graphic design software and tools. Familiarize yourself with industry-standard applications such as Adobe Creative Cloud (Illustrator, Photoshop, InDesign) to ensure you can deliver high-quality designs.

3. Create a Portfolio:

Build a strong portfolio showcasing your best design work. Feature a variety of projects that highlight your skills, style, and versatility. A compelling portfolio serves as a visual resume and helps attract potential clients.

4. Set Up a Dedicated Workspace:

Designate a dedicated workspace within your home for graphic design work. Ensure you have a comfortable and organized environment with proper lighting, ergonomic furniture, and the necessary equipment to foster creativity.

5. Legal Considerations:

Understand legal considerations for running a graphic design business from home. This may involve registering your business, obtaining necessary licenses, and establishing clear contracts for client projects. Legal compliance builds trust and credibility.

6. Online Presence:

Establish a strong online presence to attract clients. Create a professional website featuring your portfolio, services, pricing, and contact information. Utilize social media platforms to share your design work, engage with your audience, and network within the design community.

7. Network with Other Businesses:

Network with local businesses, entrepreneurs, and agencies. Attend networking events, join online forums, and collaborate with other professionals in related fields. Building connections can lead to partnerships, referrals, and a broader client base.

8. Offer Clear Services and Packages:

Clearly define your graphic design services and packages. Communicate the scope of your offerings, pricing structures, and any additional services you provide. Having clear options helps clients understand and choose the services that suit their needs.

9. Client Communication:

Prioritize effective communication with clients. Clearly understand their design requirements, provide regular updates during projects, and be responsive to feedback. Building a positive and communicative relationship with clients fosters satisfaction and repeat business.

10. Continuous Skill Enhancement:

Stay updated with the latest design trends, tools, and techniques. Attend design conferences, take online courses, and seek opportunities for continuous skill enhancement. Keeping your skills current ensures you deliver cutting-edge and relevant designs.

11. Time Management:

Develop strong time management skills to handle multiple projects efficiently. Establish clear project timelines, prioritize tasks, and communicate realistic deadlines to clients. Effective time management contributes to client satisfaction and business success.

12. Marketing Strategies:

Implement effective marketing strategies to promote your graphic design services. Utilize online advertising, create a blog showcasing your design expertise, and collaborate with influencers or businesses for cross-promotion. Marketing efforts help increase your visibility and attract new clients.

Starting a graphic design studio from home requires a blend of artistic talent, technical proficiency, and business acumen. By defining your niche, showcasing your work, and staying current with industry trends, you can create a thriving home-based graphic design business.

13

Home-based Language Tutoring

13. Home-based Language Tutoring:

Offering language tutoring services from home allows you to share your linguistic expertise and help learners achieve fluency. Here's a guide to help you establish and manage a successful home-based language tutoring business.

1. Identify Your Language Specialization:

Determine the specific language or languages you are proficient in and want to teach. Whether it's English, Spanish, French, or any other language, focusing on your strengths enhances your ability to provide effective tutoring.

2. Educational Background and Certifications:

Highlight your educational background and any relevant language certifications you may have. Communicate your proficiency in the language you teach to build trust with potential students and their parents.

3. Design a Comfortable Learning Space:

Create a comfortable and well-equipped learning space within your home. Ensure good lighting, a quiet environment, and resources such as textbooks, language learning materials, and a computer. A conducive learning space contributes to a positive educational experience.

4. Legal Considerations:

Understand and comply with legal considerations for offering language tutoring services from home. This may involve checking local regulations, obtaining necessary certifications, and adhering to any specific requirements for tutoring businesses.

5. Online or In-Person Tutoring:

Decide whether you'll offer in-person tutoring, online sessions, or a combination of both. With the availability of online learning platforms, having the flexibility to cater to different preferences can expand your reach and accommodate diverse student needs.

6. Customized Lesson Plans:

Create customized lesson plans for each student based on their proficiency level, goals, and learning style. Tailoring your approach ensures that students receive targeted support, leading to improved language skills.

7. Set Clear Pricing and Policies:

Define your pricing structure and policies for cancellations, rescheduling, and payment methods. Clear communication about costs and expectations helps build a professional and transparent relationship with students and their parents.

8. Utilize Language Learning Apps:

Incorporate language learning apps and online resources to enhance your tutoring sessions. These tools can supplement your teaching methods, provide interactive exercises, and engage students in the language learning process.

9. Marketing Strategies:

Implement effective marketing strategies to attract language learners. Create a professional website with details about your tutoring services, educational background, and testimonials. Utilize local advertising, social media, and partnerships with language learning communities to reach your target audience.

10. Networking with Language Communities:

Network with local language communities, cultural centers, and language exchange groups. Establishing connections can lead to referrals and collaborations. Participating in language-related events or activities helps you become a valuable resource within these communities.

11. Continuous Professional Development:

Stay informed about language teaching methodologies, resources, and cultural nuances. Attend language education conferences, participate in workshops, and explore opportunities for continuous professional development. Staying updated ensures your tutoring methods remain effective and engaging.

12. Feedback and Improvement:

Encourage feedback from your students and their parents. Use constructive feedback to continually improve your teaching methods and address any areas of improvement. A commitment to ongoing improvement enhances the quality of your language tutoring services.

13. Cultural Sensitivity:

Be culturally sensitive in your language tutoring. Understand and respect cultural differences, incorporating cultural elements into your lessons. This fosters a deeper appreciation for the language and enriches the overall learning experience for your students.

Establishing a home-based language tutoring business requires a combination of linguistic expertise, effective teaching methods, and a commitment to continuous improvement. By creating a comfortable learning environment, customizing lessons, and staying connected with language communities, you can help students achieve language proficiency and build a successful tutoring business.

65

14

Virtual Assistant Services:

14. Virtual Assistant Services:

Offering virtual assistant services from home allows you to provide administrative support to businesses and entrepreneurs remotely. Here's a guide to help you establish and manage a successful home-based virtual assistant business.

1. Define Your Services:

Clearly outline the virtual assistant services you offer. This may include tasks such as email management, scheduling, data entry, social media management, and more. Specify your expertise to attract clients with specific needs.

2. Set Up a Professional Workspace:

Create a dedicated and organized workspace within your home for virtual assistant work. Ensure you have a reliable computer, high-speed internet, and necessary software tools to efficiently carry out your tasks. A professional workspace contributes to productivity and professionalism.

3. Develop a Skill Set:

Build a versatile skill set that aligns with the needs of virtual assistant clients. Stay proficient in communication tools, project management software, and other platforms commonly used in virtual collaboration. Continuous learning enhances your capabilities.

4. Legal Considerations:

Understand legal considerations for offering virtual assistant services. This may include business registration, contracts, and compliance with data protection regulations. Ensure that your business practices adhere to legal standards and protect both you and your clients.

5. Online Presence:

Establish a strong online presence to attract clients. Create a professional website detailing your virtual assistant services, skills, and contact information. Utilize platforms like

LinkedIn and social media to showcase your expertise and connect with potential clients.

6. Client Onboarding Process:

Develop a streamlined client onboarding process. Clearly communicate your services, pricing structure, and terms of engagement. Providing a smooth onboarding experience sets the tone for a successful working relationship with your clients.

7. Time Management and Efficiency:

Master time management techniques to handle multiple tasks efficiently. Use project management tools to track deadlines, prioritize tasks, and ensure timely delivery of services. Demonstrating efficiency enhances your reputation as a reliable virtual assistant.

8. Networking with Entrepreneurs and Businesses:

Network with entrepreneurs, small businesses, and other professionals in need of virtual assistant services. Join online communities, attend virtual networking events, and collaborate with other freelancers to expand your client base.

9. Confidentiality and Trust:

Prioritize confidentiality and trust in your virtual assistant services. Handle sensitive information securely, and communicate your commitment to client privacy. Building trust with clients is essential for maintaining long-term working relationships.

10. Pricing Structure:

Develop a transparent pricing structure for your virtual assistant services. Consider hourly rates, retainer packages, or project-based pricing. Clearly communicate your rates and the value clients receive for their investment in your services.

11. Communication Skills:

Cultivate strong communication skills. Respond promptly to client messages, provide clear updates on tasks, and establish effective communication channels. Proactive and clear communication enhances your professionalism and client satisfaction.

12. Continuous Learning and Adaptability:

Stay updated with the latest tools, technology, and trends in virtual assistance. Continuous learning and adaptability ensure that your services remain relevant and can evolve to meet changing client needs.

Starting a home-based virtual assistant business requires a combination of organizational skills, technical proficiency, and effective communication. By offering specialized services, maintaining professionalism, and continuously improving your skills, you can build a successful virtual assistant business that caters to the needs of businesses and entrepreneurs.

15

Home-based E-commerce Store

15. Home-based E-commerce Store:

Setting up an e-commerce store from home allows you to sell products online and reach a global audience. Here's a guide to help you establish and manage a successful home-based e-commerce business.

1. Choose Your Niche:Identify a niche or product category that aligns with your interests and has market demand. Focusing on a specific niche allows you to stand out and target a particular audience.

2. Source or Create Products:Decide whether you'll source existing products or create your own. Research suppliers, manufacturers, or consider crafting handmade items. Ensure the quality and uniqueness of your products to attract customers.

3. Set Up Your Online Store:Create a professional and user-friendly online store. Use e-commerce platforms like Shopify, WooCommerce, or Etsy to set up your store. Include high-quality product images, detailed descriptions, and an easy checkout process.

4. Legal Compliance:Understand and comply with legal requirements for operating an e-commerce store. This may include business registration, obtaining necessary licenses, and compliance with consumer protection laws. Ensure secure payment processing and protect customer data.

5. Payment and Shipping Setup: Set up secure payment gateways and clearly communicate your shipping policies. Provide various payment options to accommodate customer preferences. Offer transparent shipping rates, estimated delivery times, and tracking information.

6. Build Your Brand:Develop a strong brand identity for your e-commerce store. Create a memorable logo, use consistent branding across your website and marketing materials, and tell a compelling story about your products. Building a brand fosters trust and loyalty.

7. Online Marketing Strategies:Implement effective online marketing strategies to drive traffic to your e-commerce

store. Utilize social media advertising, content marketing, and email campaigns to promote your products. Consider collaborations with influencers or affiliates to expand your reach.

8. Customer Service Excellence:Prioritize exceptional customer service. Respond promptly to customer inquiries, address issues or concerns, and provide a positive buying experience. Positive customer interactions lead to repeat business and positive reviews.

9. SEO Optimization:Optimize your e-commerce store for search engines. Conduct keyword research, optimize product listings, and utilize SEO techniques to improve your store's visibility in search engine results. Effective SEO increases your chances of reaching a broader audience.

10. Utilize Analytics:Use analytics tools to track and analyze website traffic, customer behavior, and sales data. Gain insights into customer preferences, popular products, and areas for improvement. Data-driven decision-making enhances the performance of your e-commerce store.

11. Sales Promotions and Discounts:Implement sales promotions, discounts, or special offers to attract customers. Consider launching promotions during peak seasons,

holidays, or to celebrate milestones. Promotions can drive sales and create a sense of urgency among buyers.

12. Expand Product Range:Regularly assess market trends and customer feedback to expand your product range. Introduce new products or variations to keep your store fresh and appealing. Diversifying your offerings can attract a wider customer base.

13. Responsive Customer Feedback:

Encourage customer feedback and reviews. Display positive reviews on your website to build trust with potential customers. Responsively address any negative feedback to demonstrate your commitment to customer satisfaction.

14. Sustainable Practices:Consider incorporating sustainable practices into your e-commerce business. Use eco-friendly packaging, source products responsibly, and communicate your commitment to sustainability. This can attract environmentally conscious customers.

15. Stay Informed about E-commerce Trends:Stay informed about emerging trends in e-commerce. Attend industry conferences, follow industry blogs, and participate in relevant forums. Adapting to changing trends ensures your e-commerce store remains competitive and relevant.

Starting a home-based e-commerce store requires strategic planning, attention to customer experience, and adaptability to market trends. By offering quality products, building a strong brand, and leveraging effective marketing strategies, you can create a successful and sustainable e-commerce business from the comfort of your home.